Peggy Louise Parrish
Parma, Idaho 83660

The drawings and writing in the interior and on the cover of this book re by
Peggy Louise Parrish

ISBN- 13: 978-1543207927
Printed in The United States of America

The Incredible Letter I

Coloring Book

By Peggy Louise Parrish

C. 2017

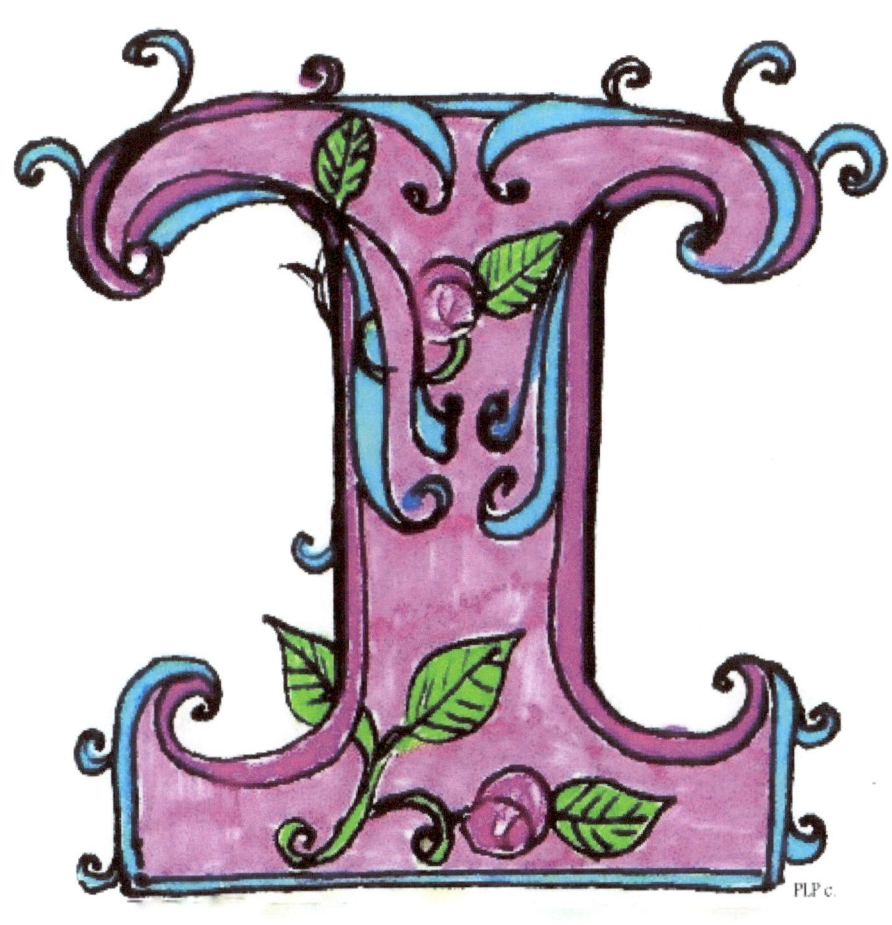

PLP c.

Welcome to an Incredible Letter I Adventure!

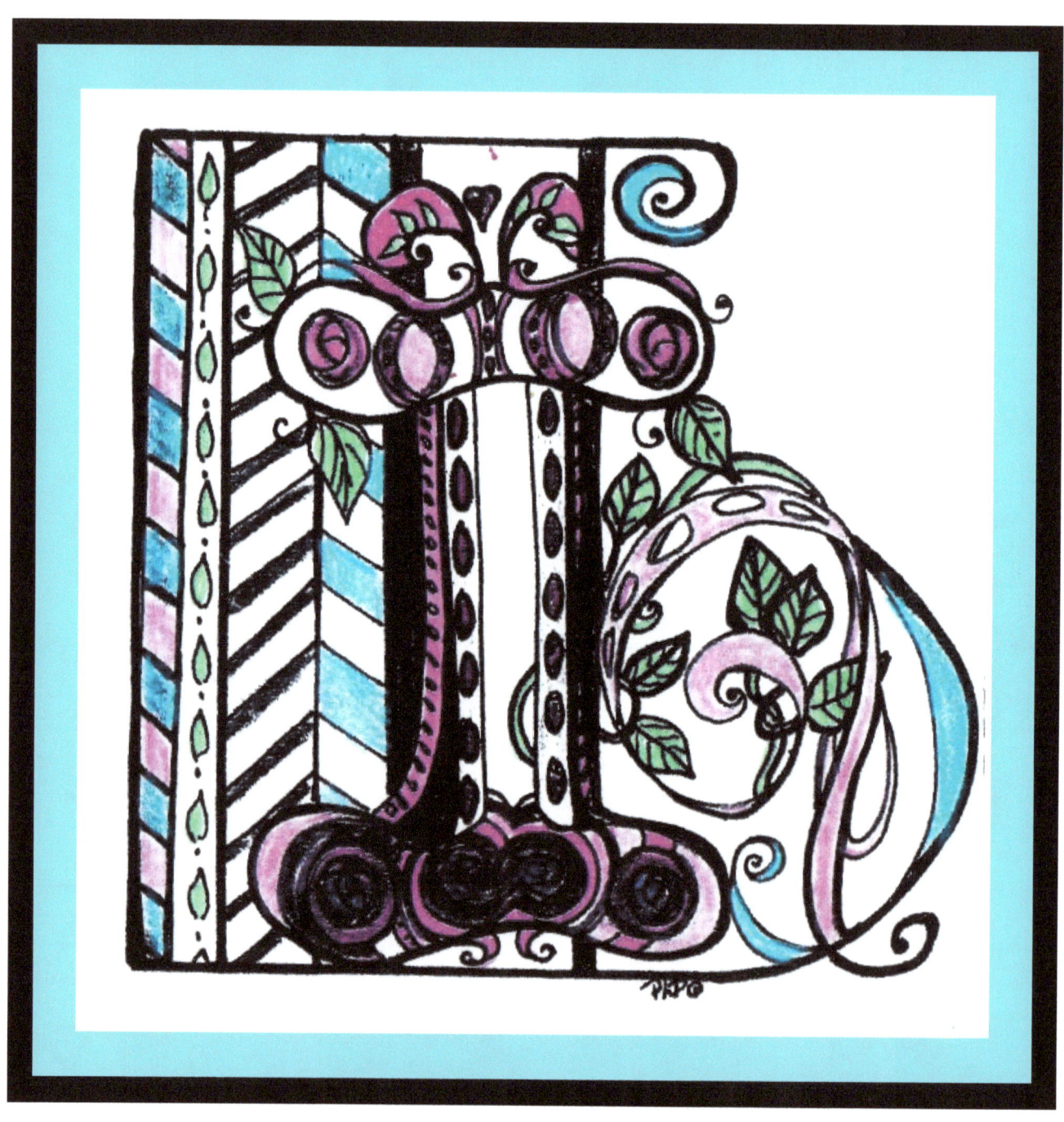

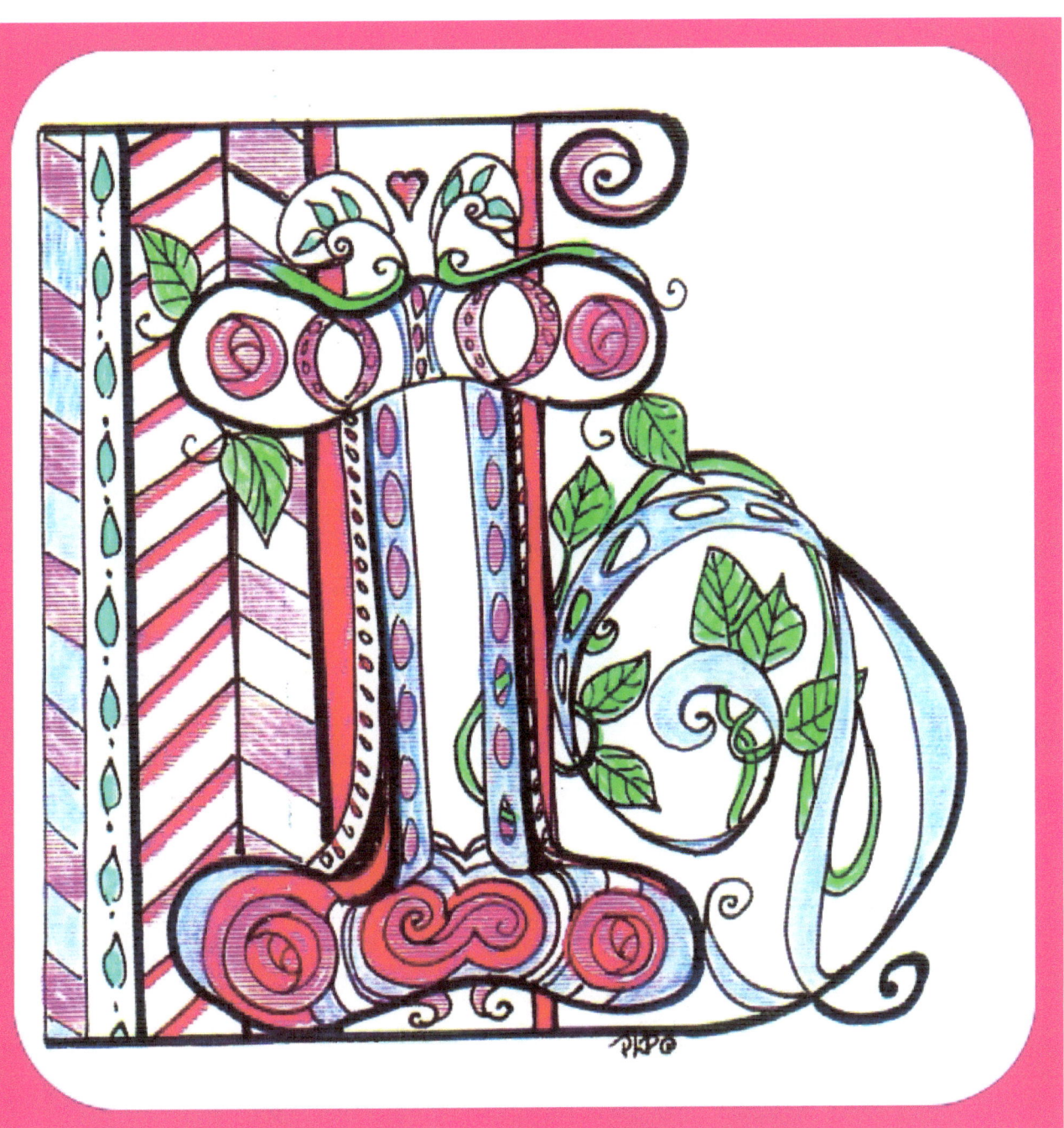

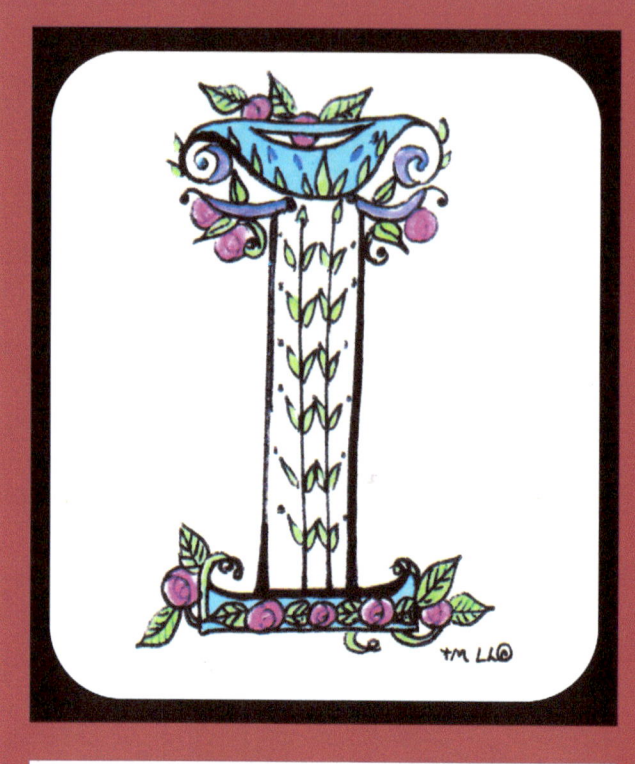

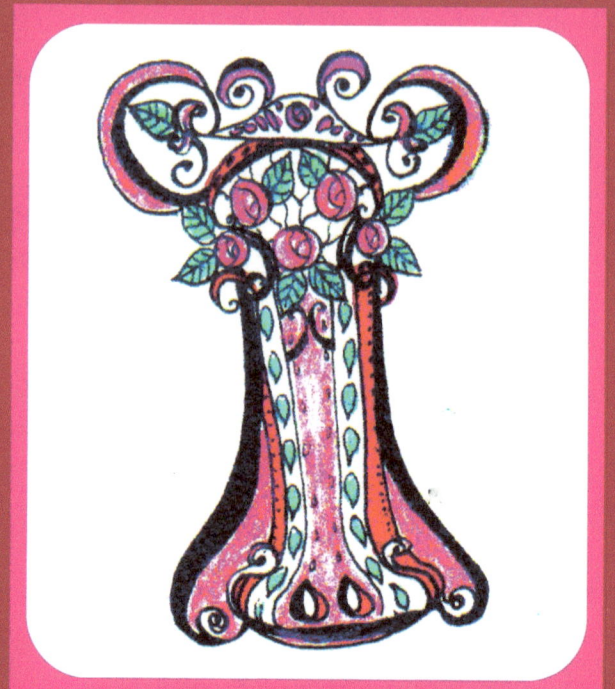

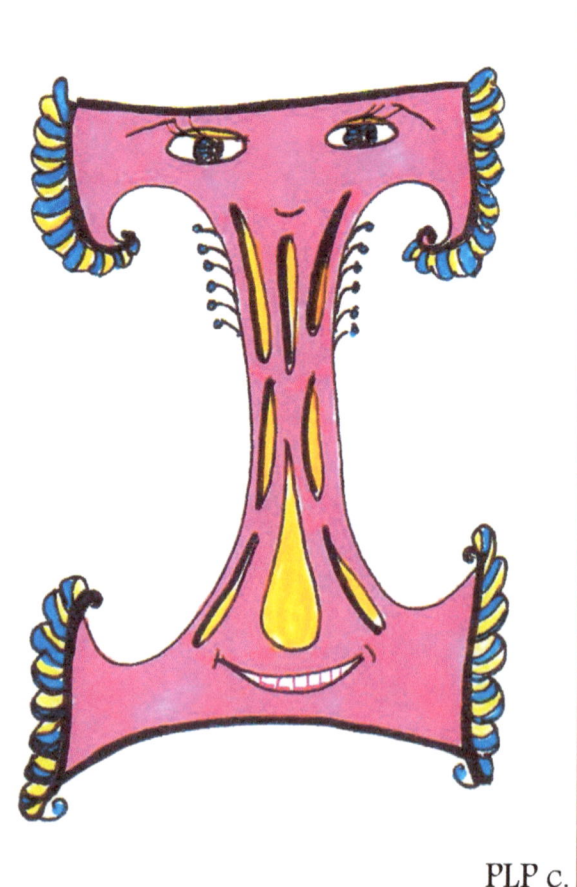

PLP c.

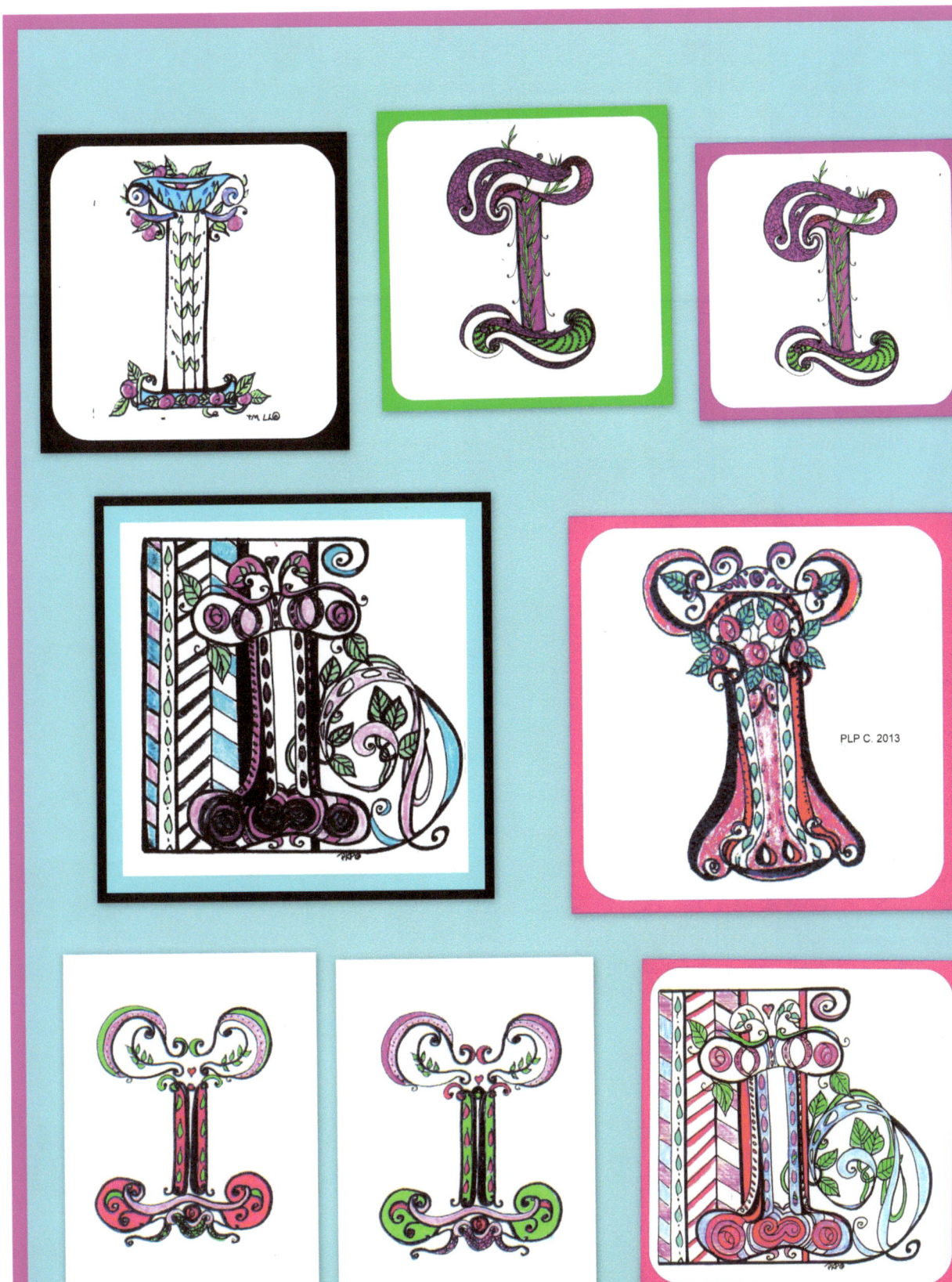

Welcome to an adventure with letter I. Artist Peggy Louise Parrish has designed these letters for both herself and others to color. There will be some you like better than others. You may make a few "in house" copies of the ones you like the most to color in several ways. Make sure you keep her initials on the pages. You may use them to display or give as gifts. Perhaps your first or last name begins with the letter I. Or maybe you would like to start a word with a fancy I. Hopefully you will have a lot of fun discovering the possibilities with your choice of colors.

Quality colored pencils are the preferred medium used on these pages. If however, you would like to use gel pens, markers, paint or watercolor pencils place a scrap paper under your work. In these pages are a few examples of color choices. The real fun lies in choosing your own. Just for fun you may want to glitter a few.

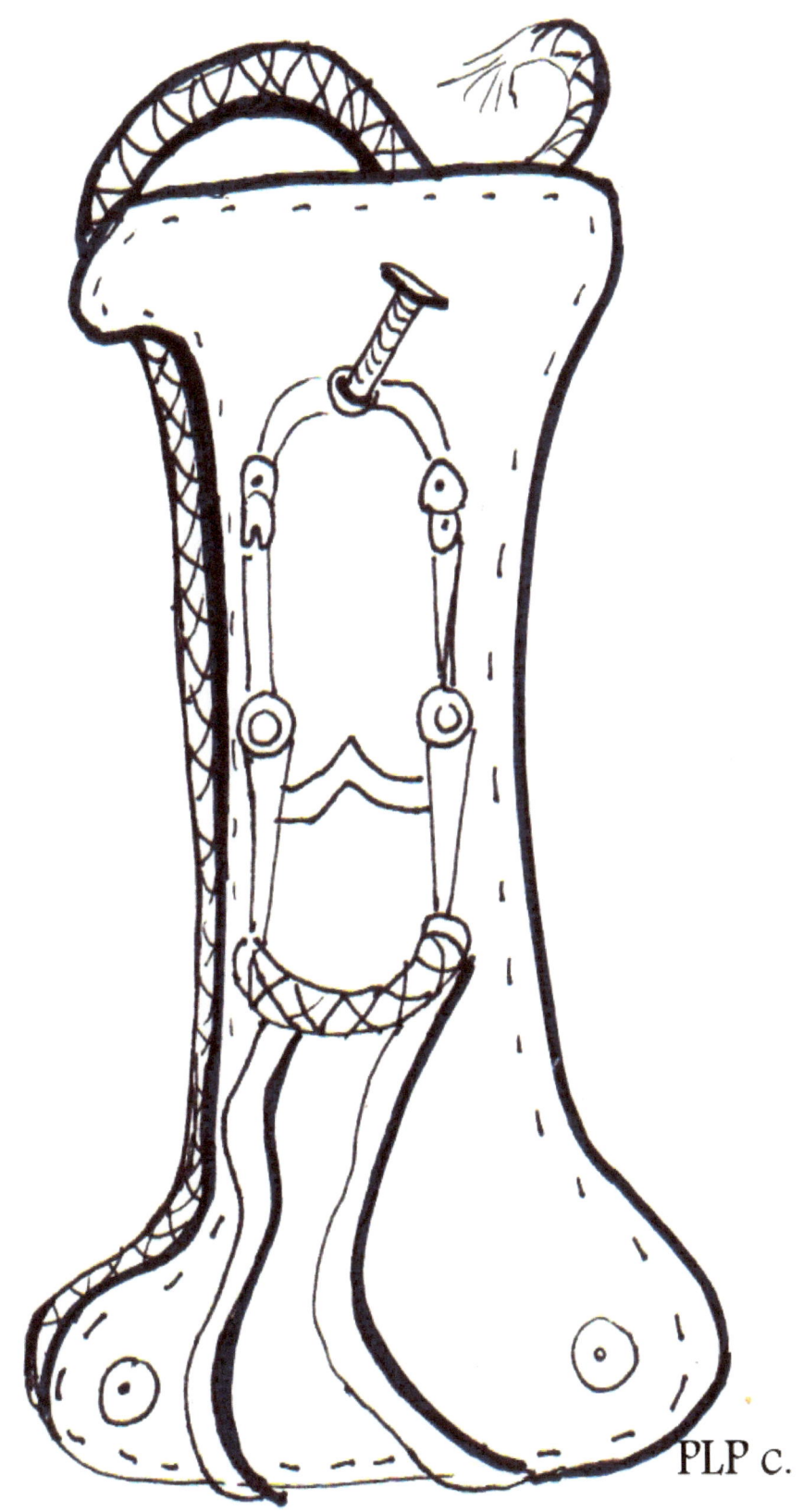

PLP c.

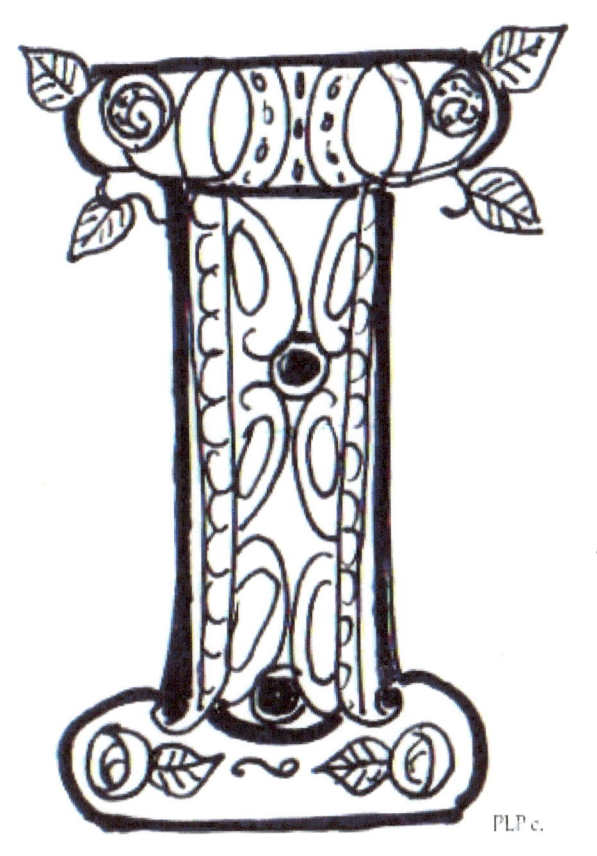

PLP c.

PLP c.

19

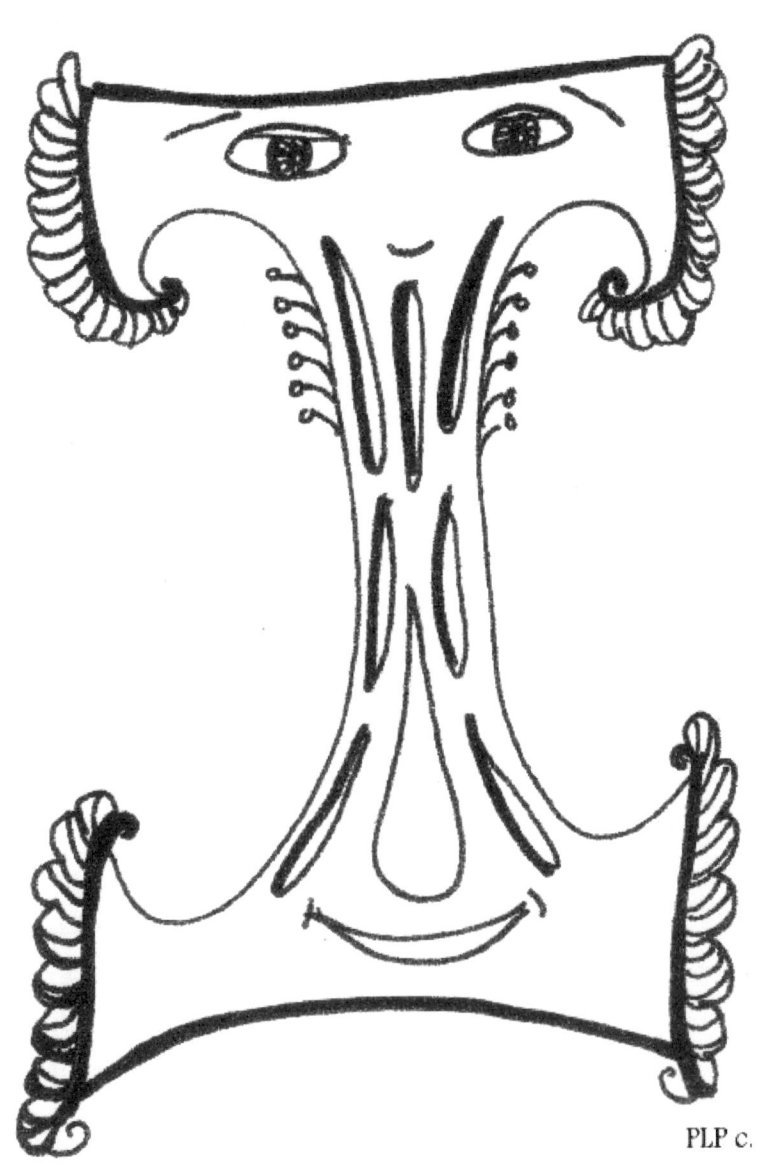

PLP c.

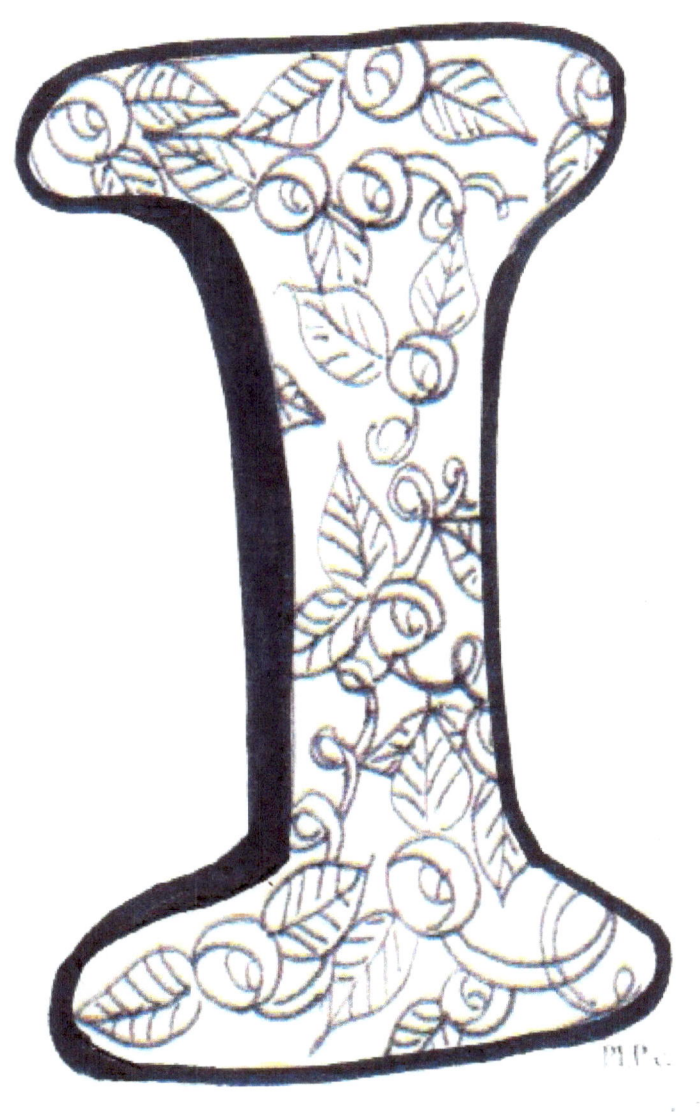

23

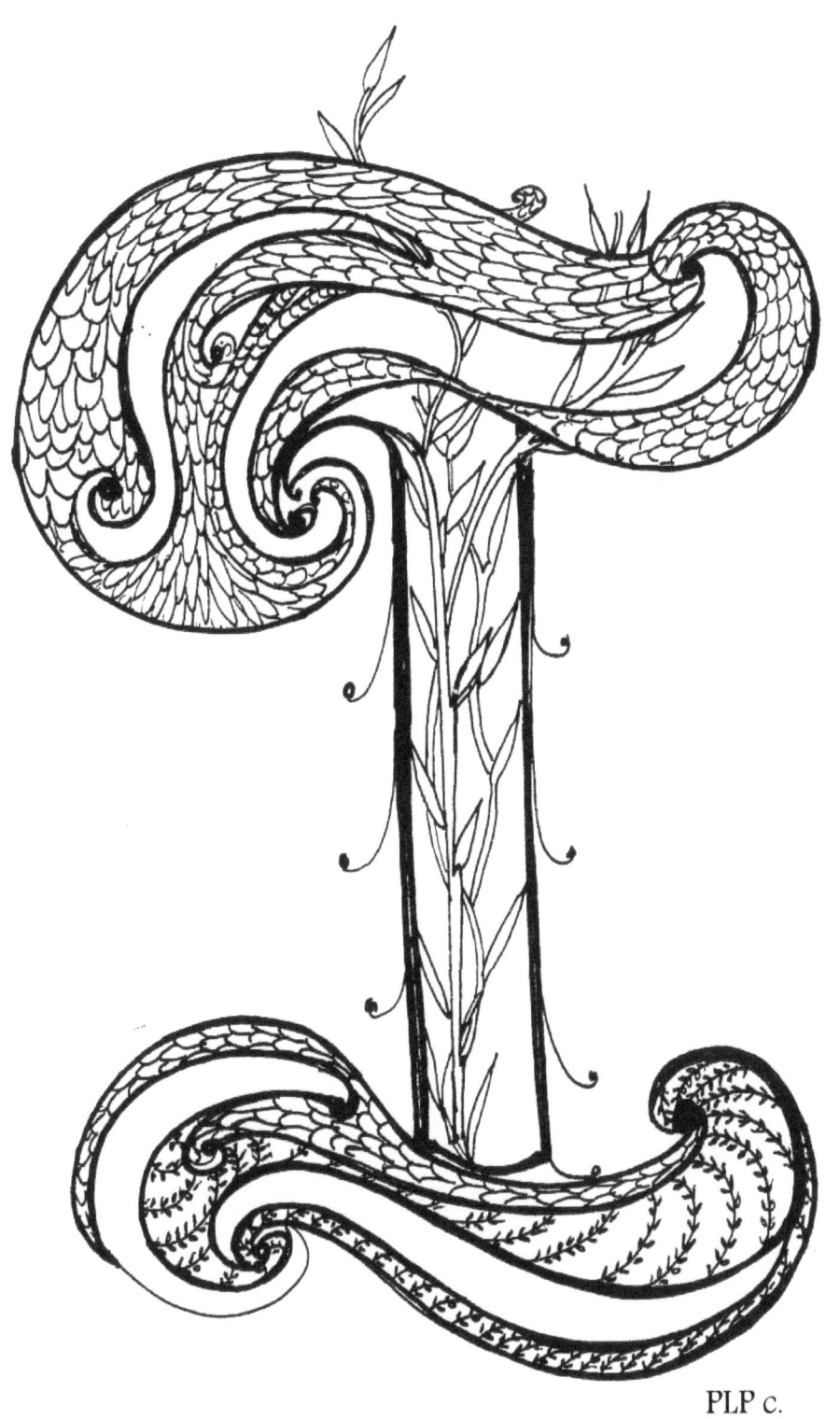

PLP c.

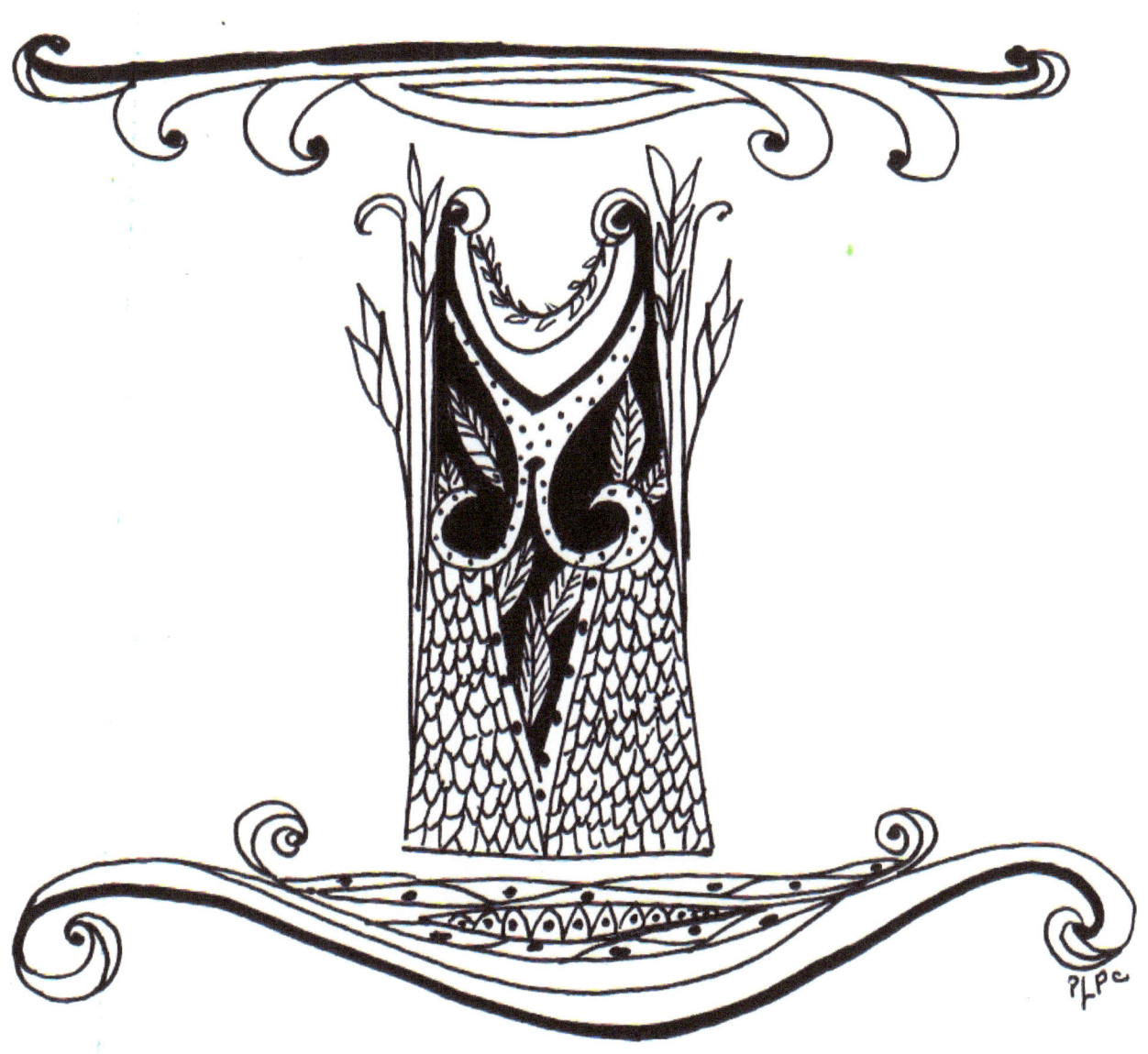

27

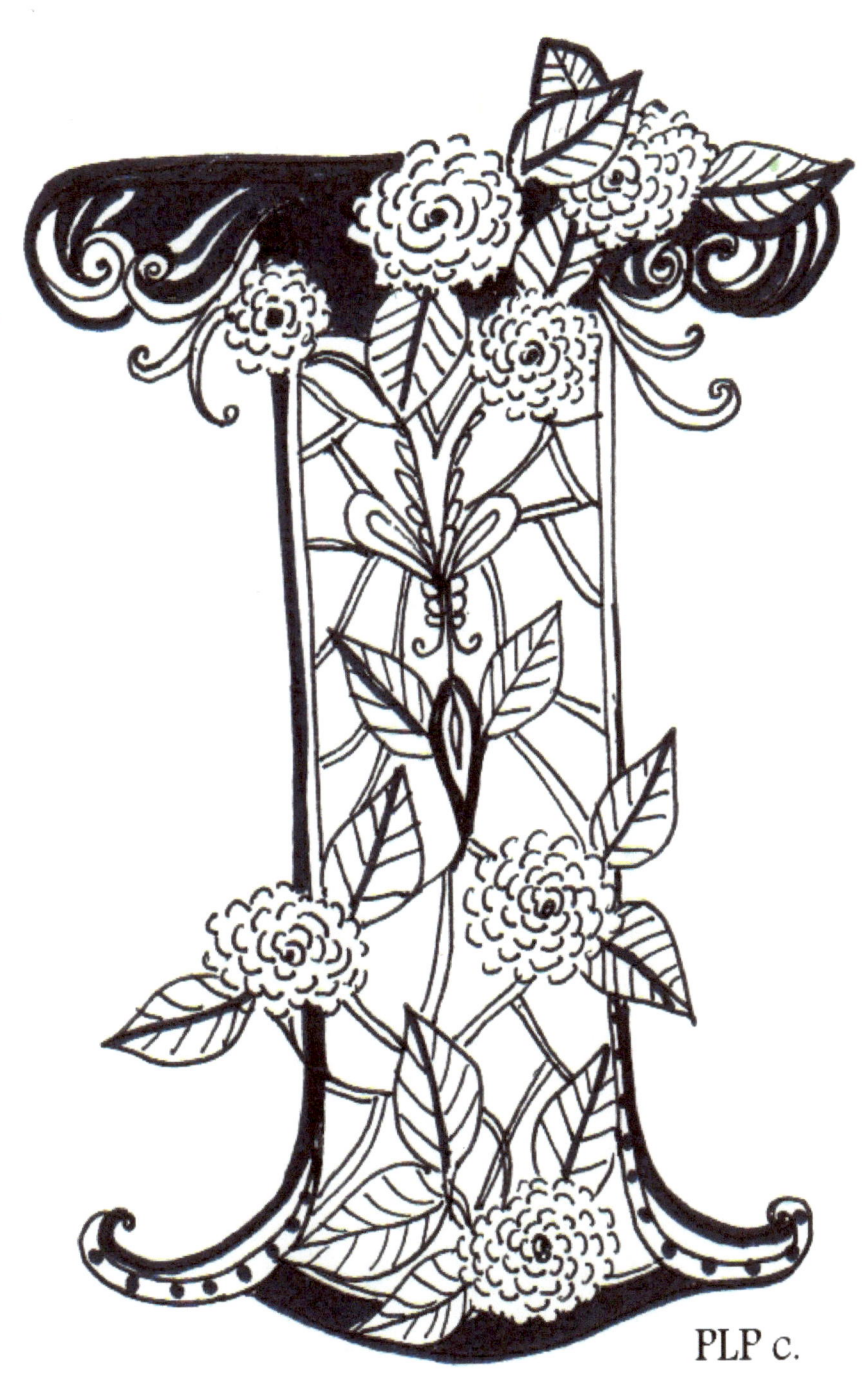

PLP c.

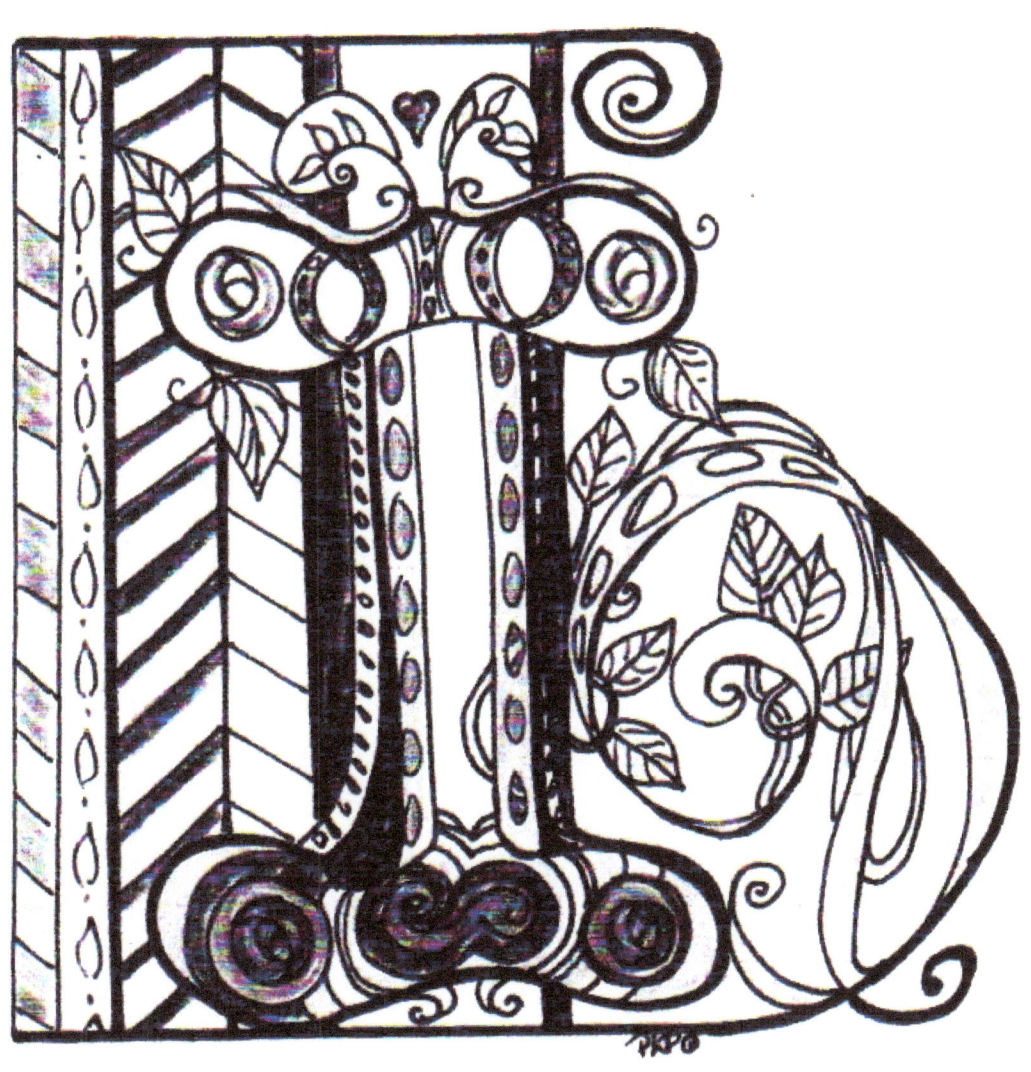

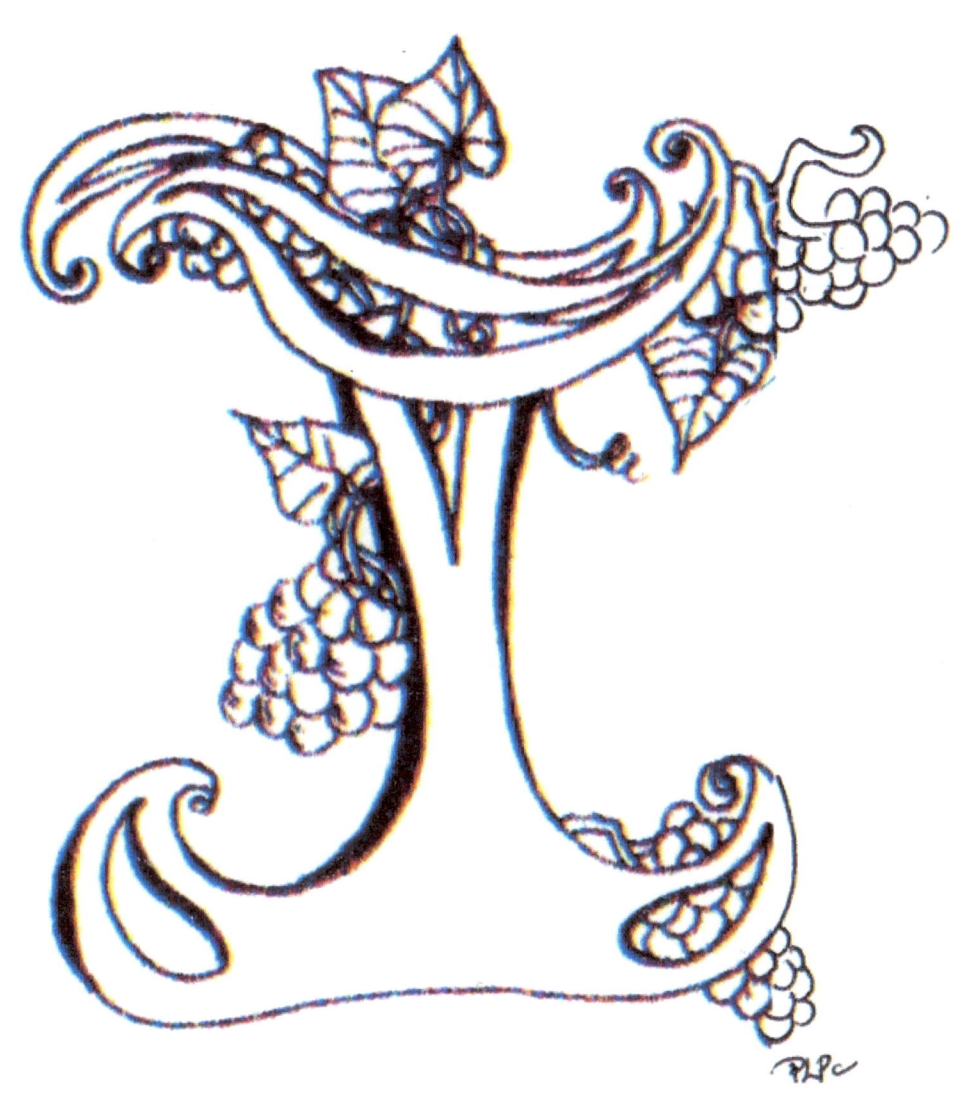

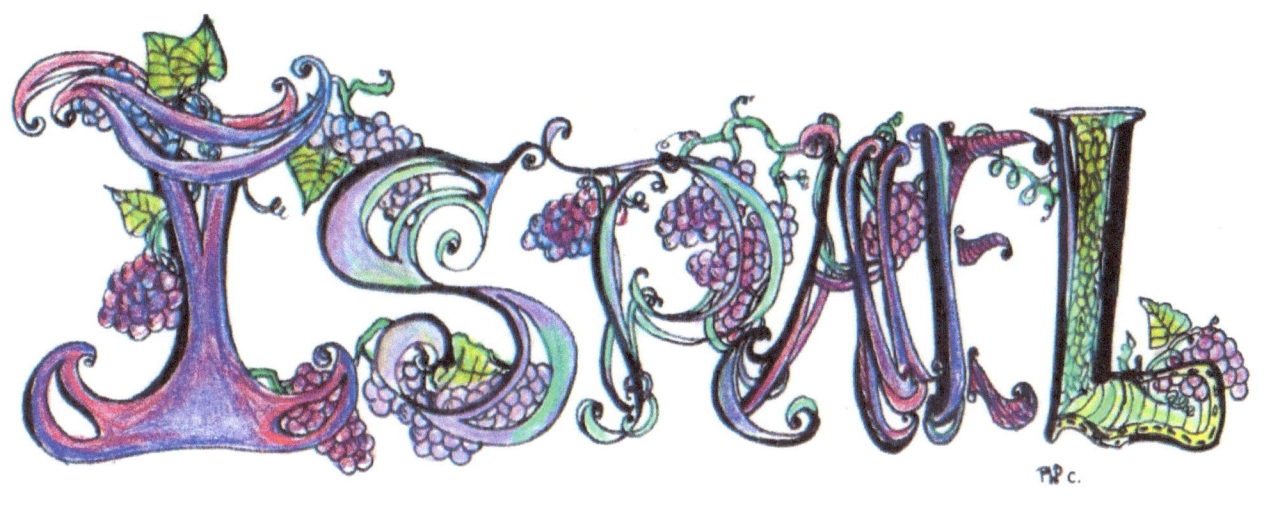

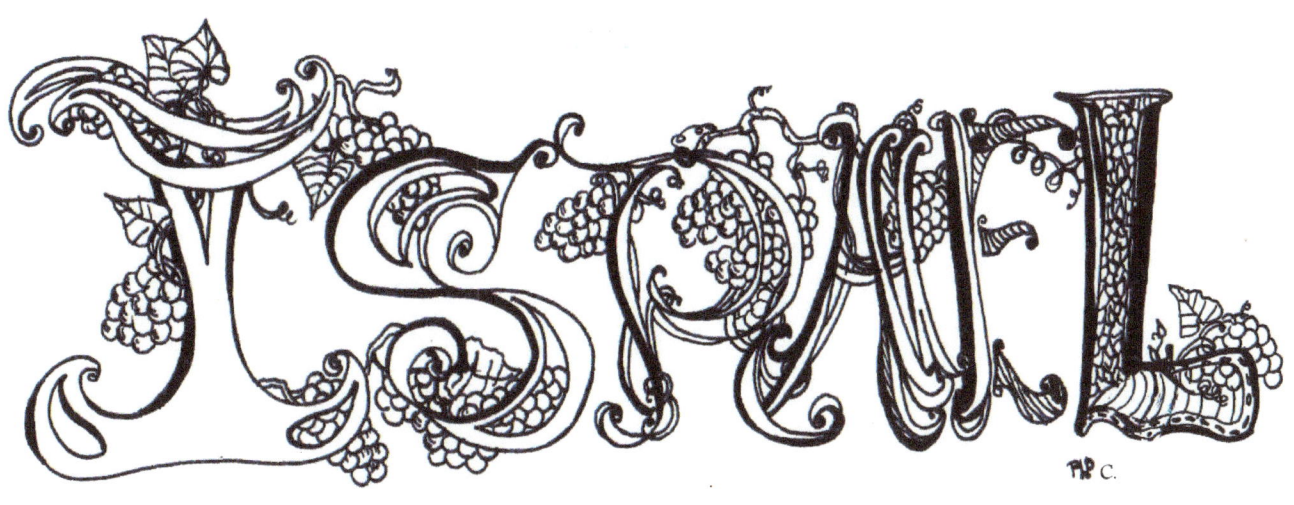

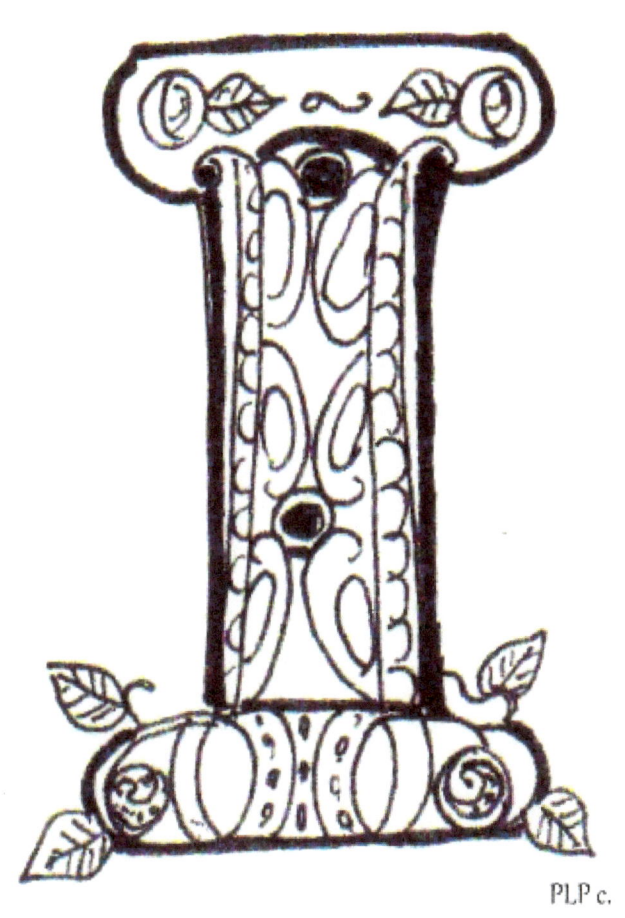

PLP c.

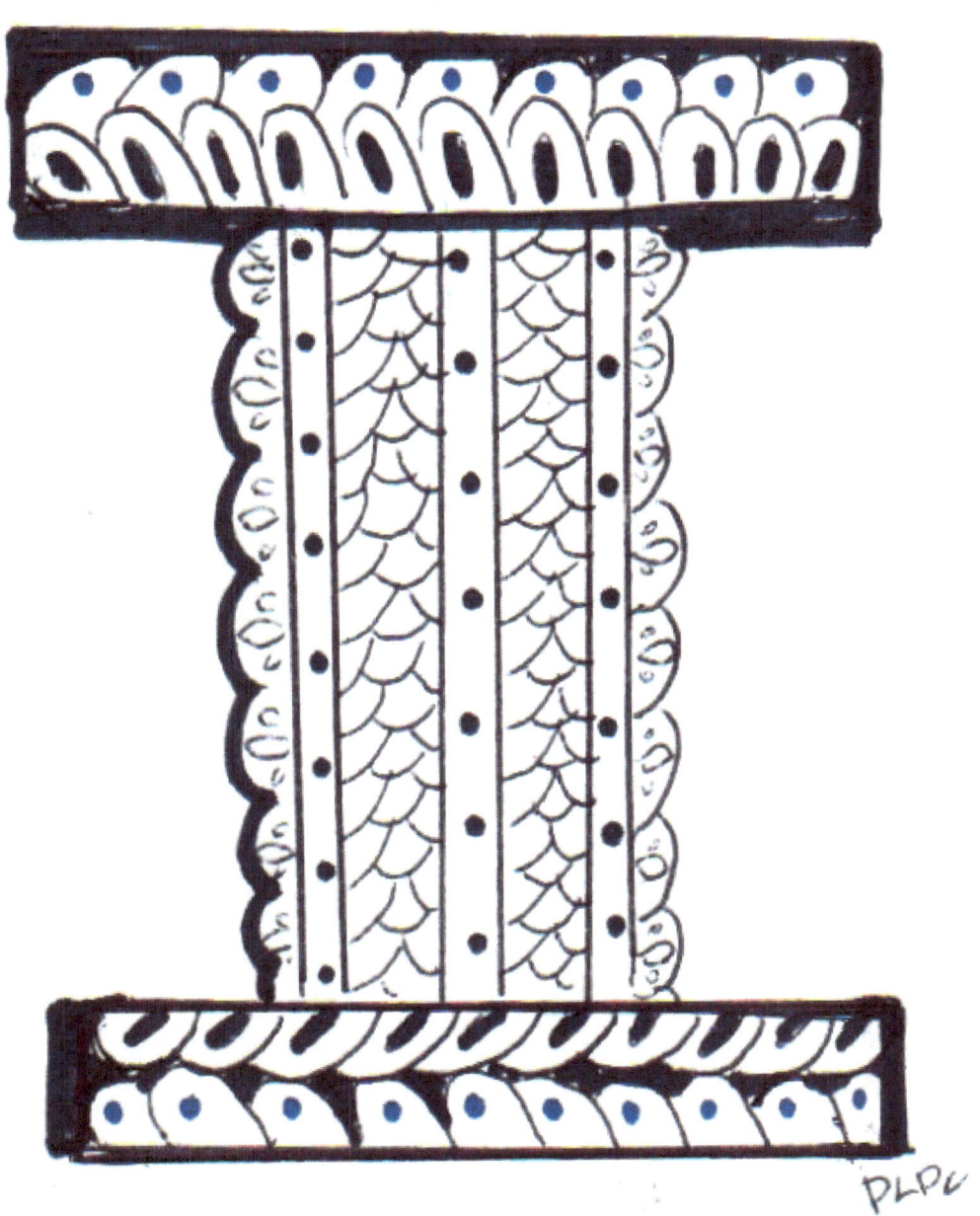

PLPC

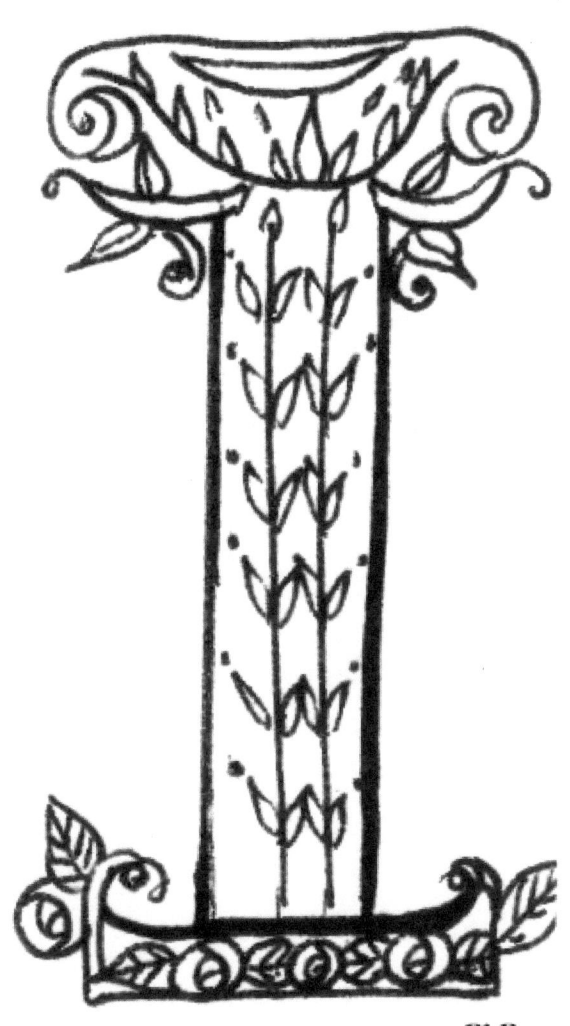

PLP c.

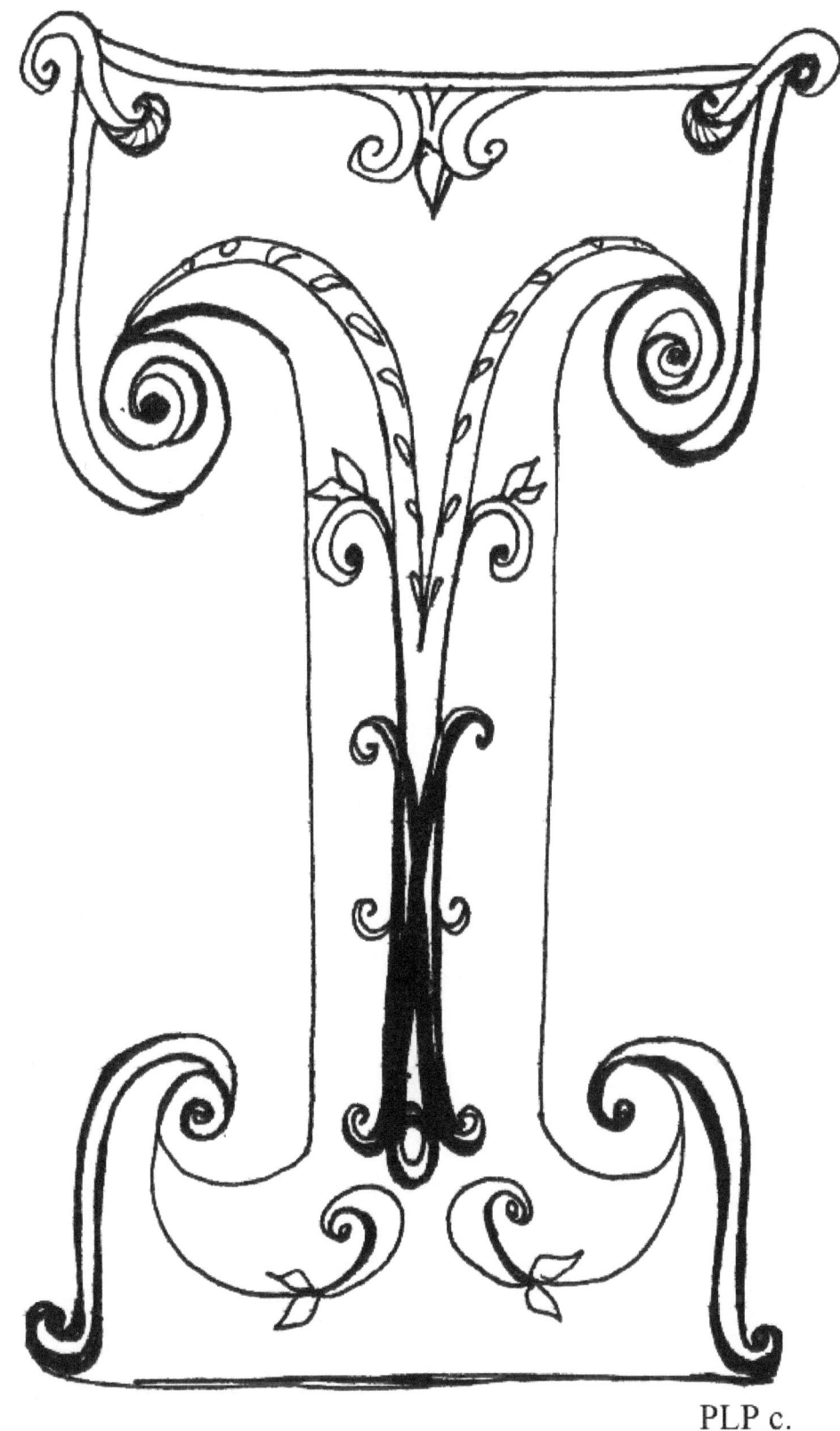

PLP c.

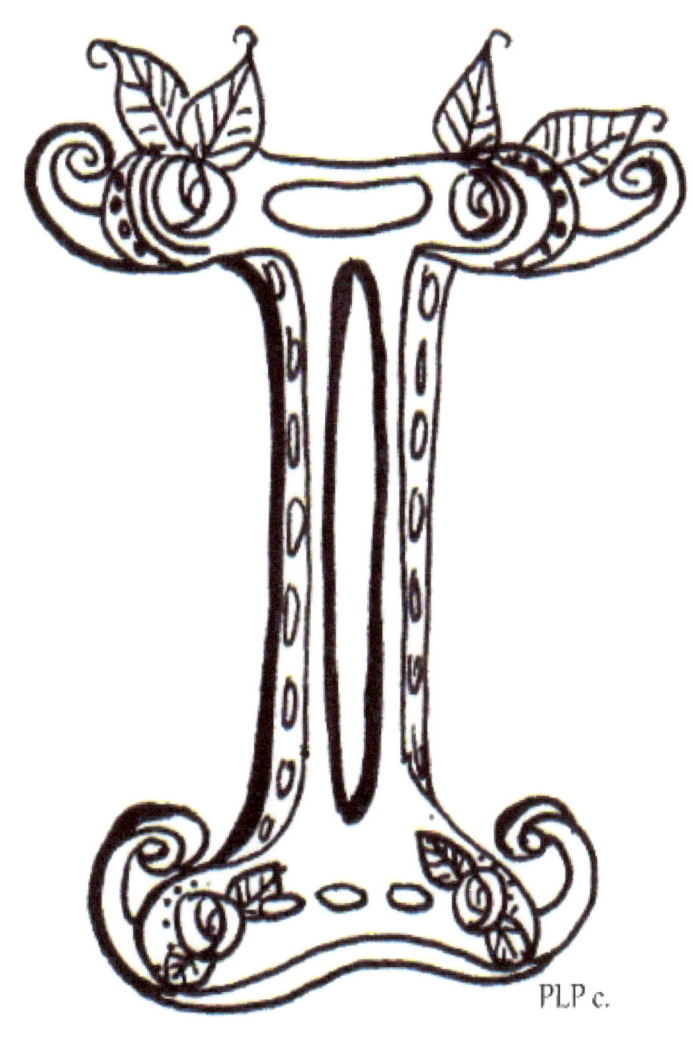

PLP c.

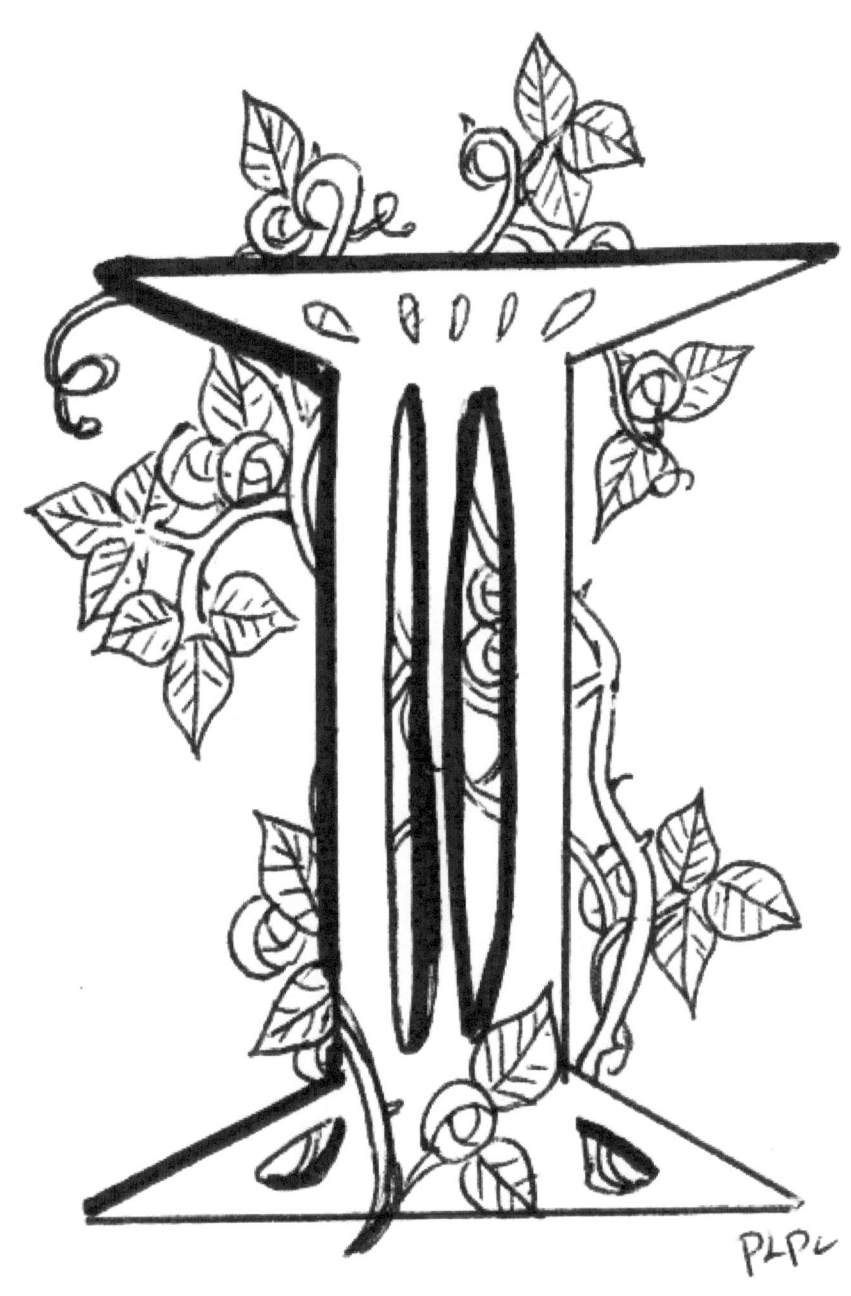

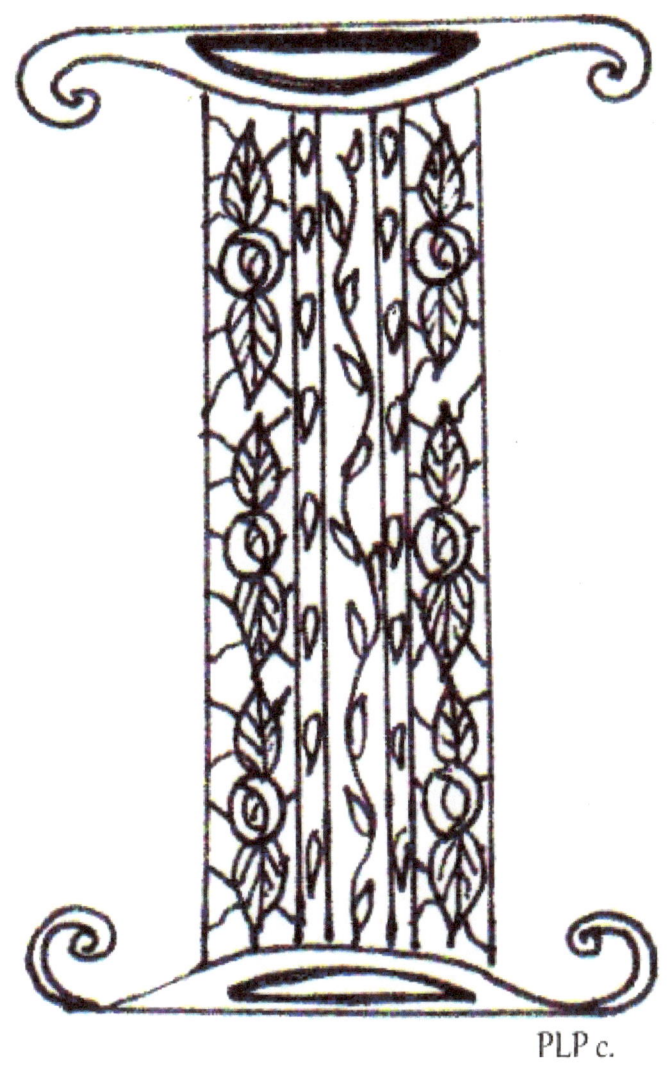

PLP c.

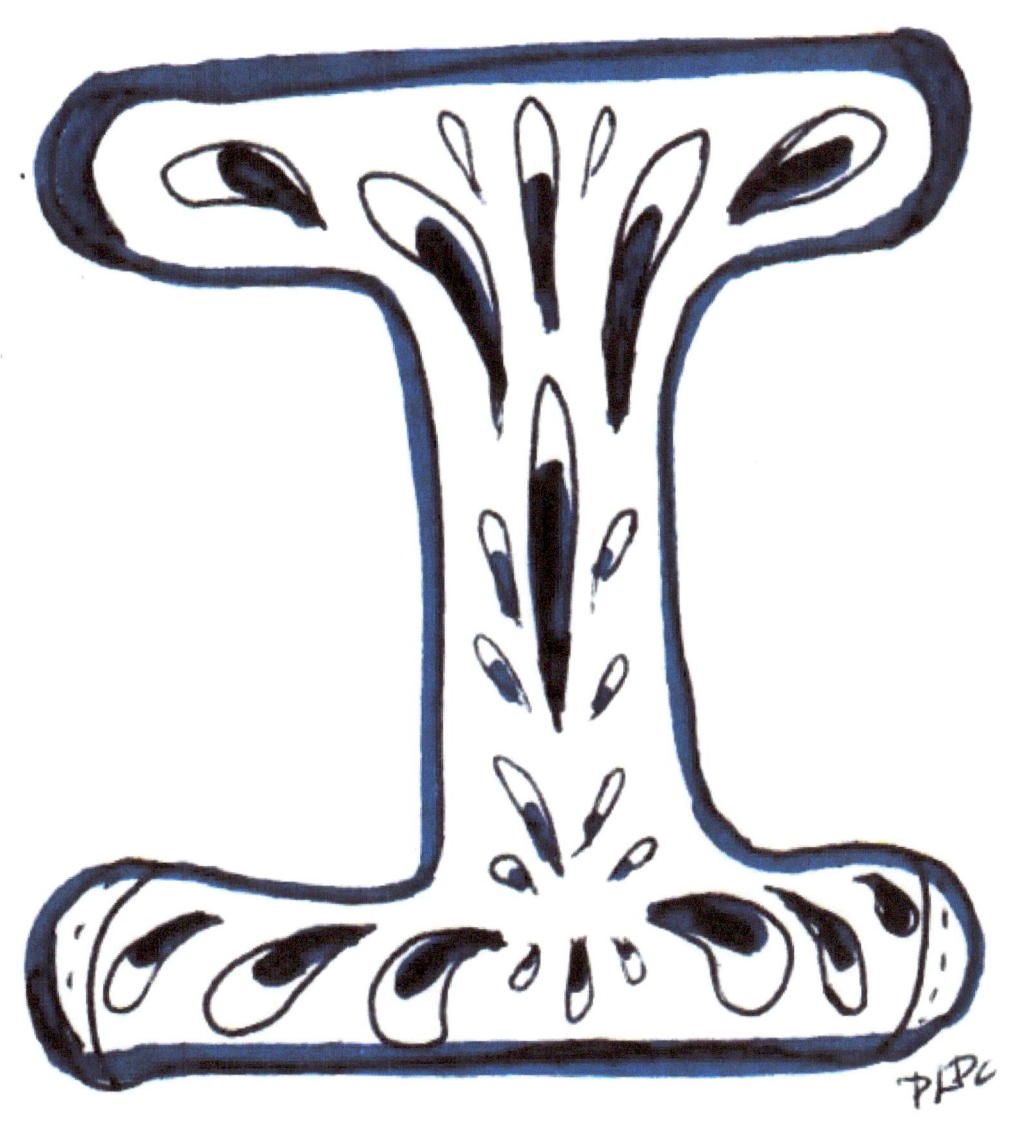

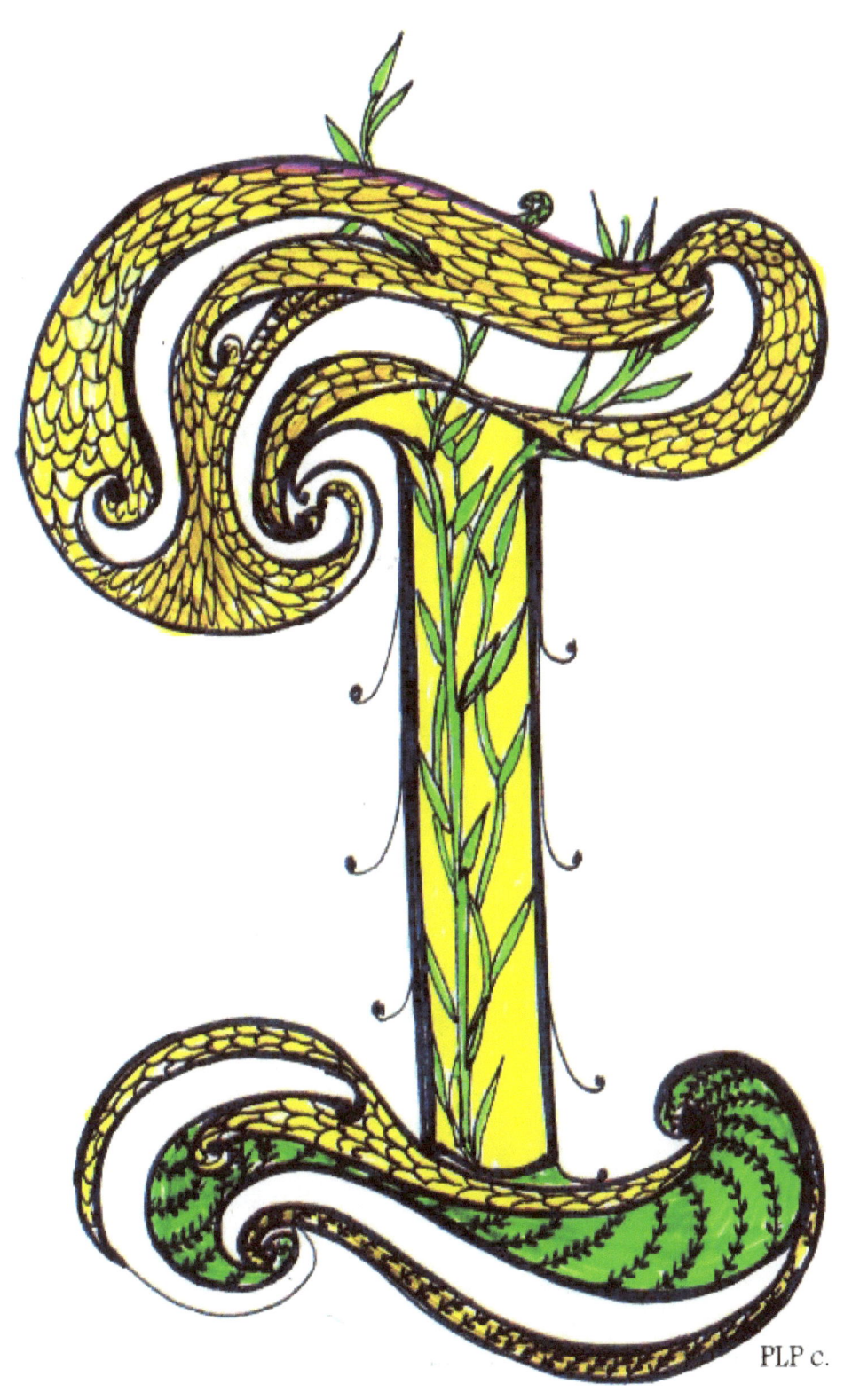

PLP c.

This I sure likes the color Blue!

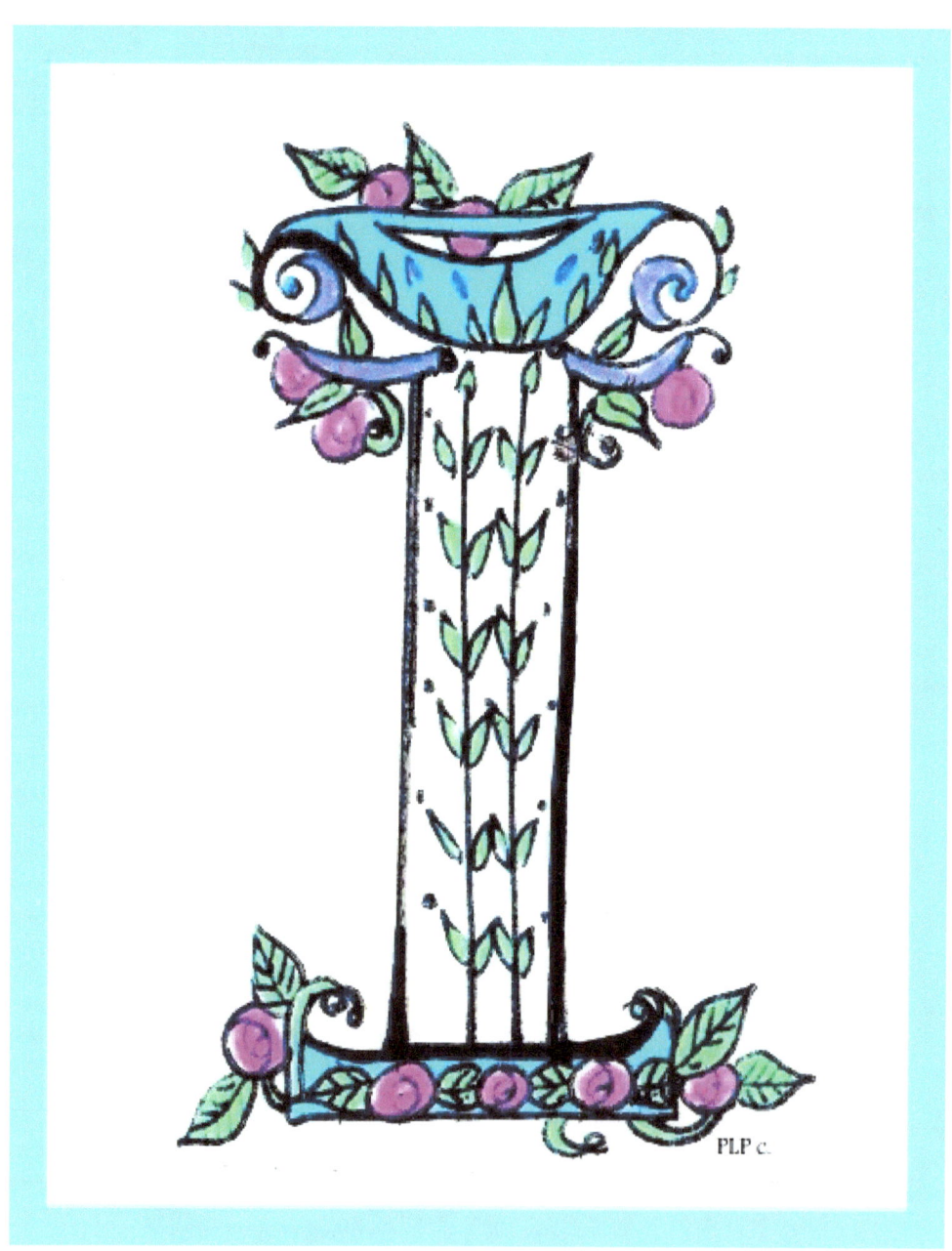

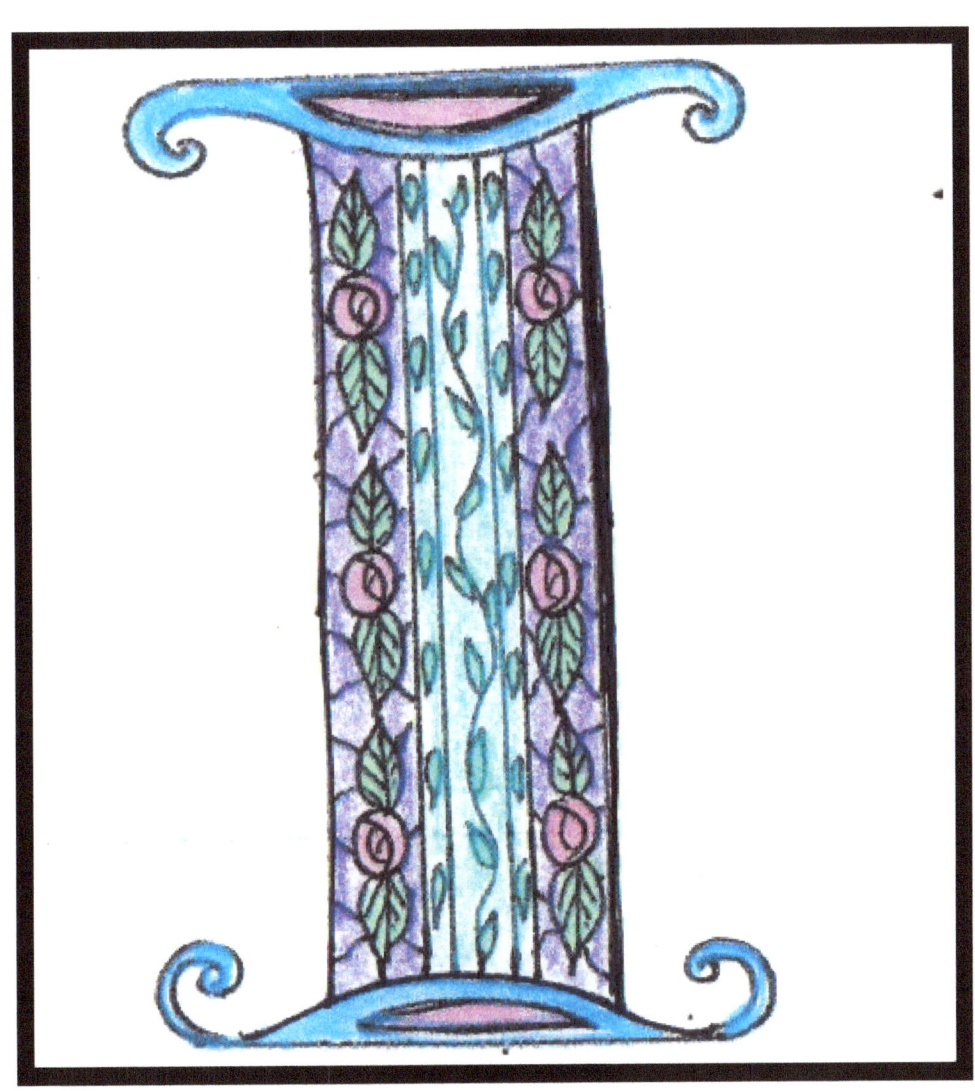

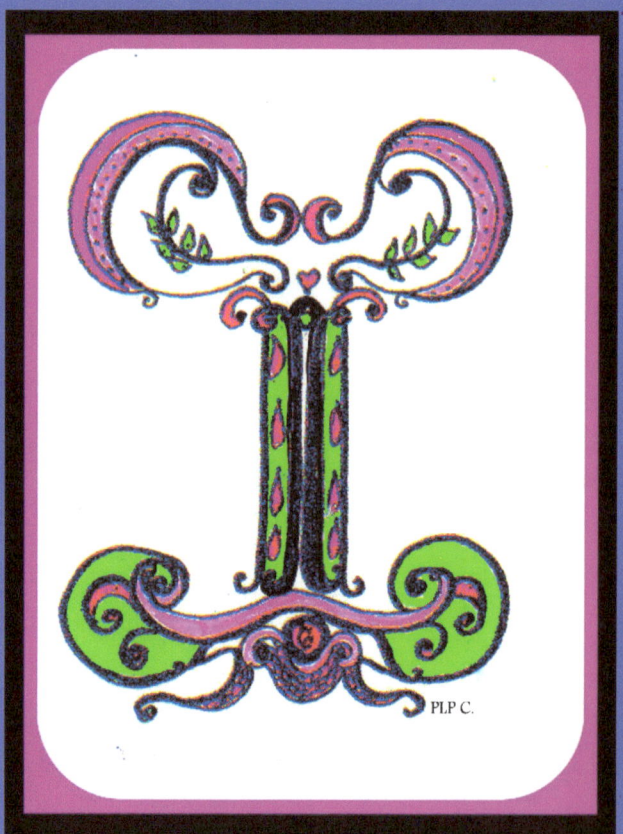
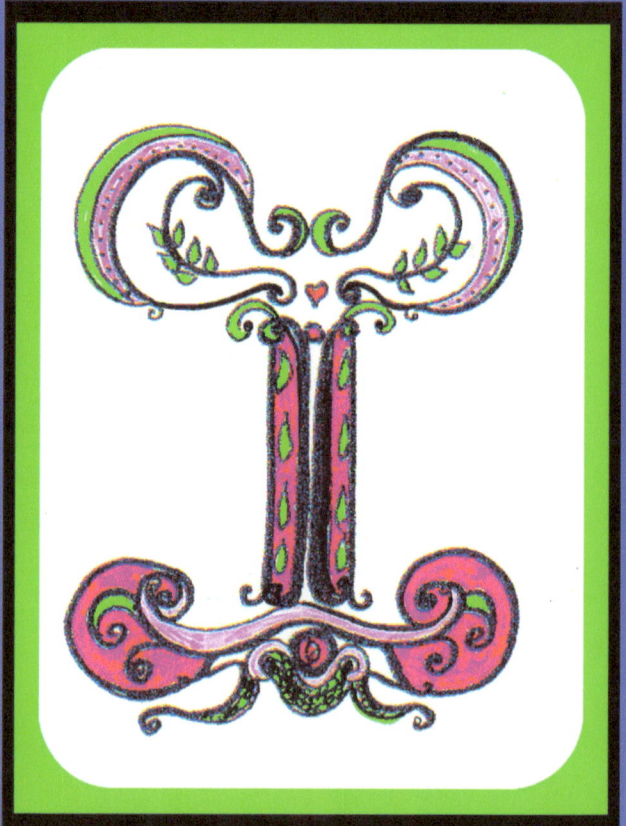

PLP C.

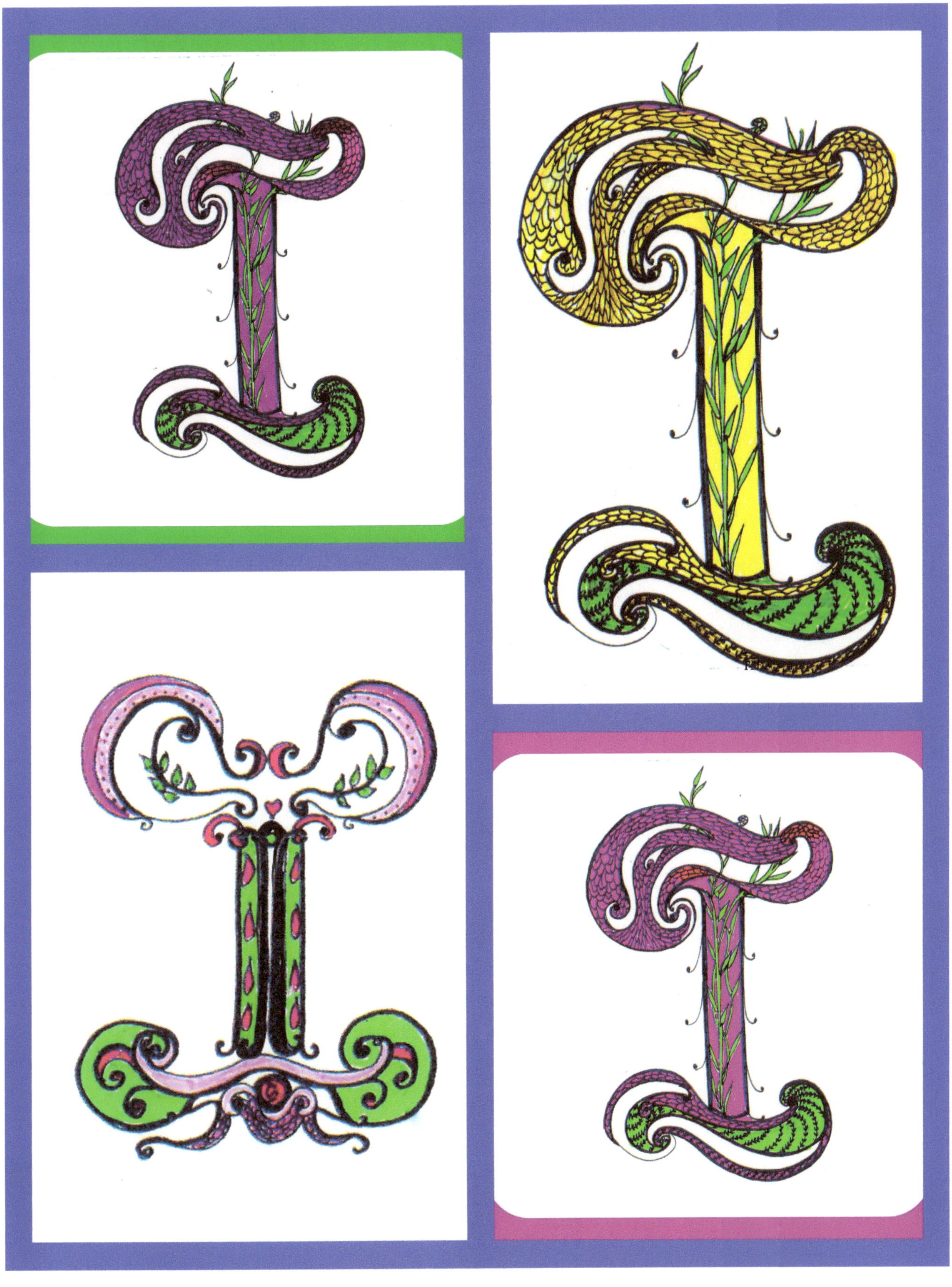

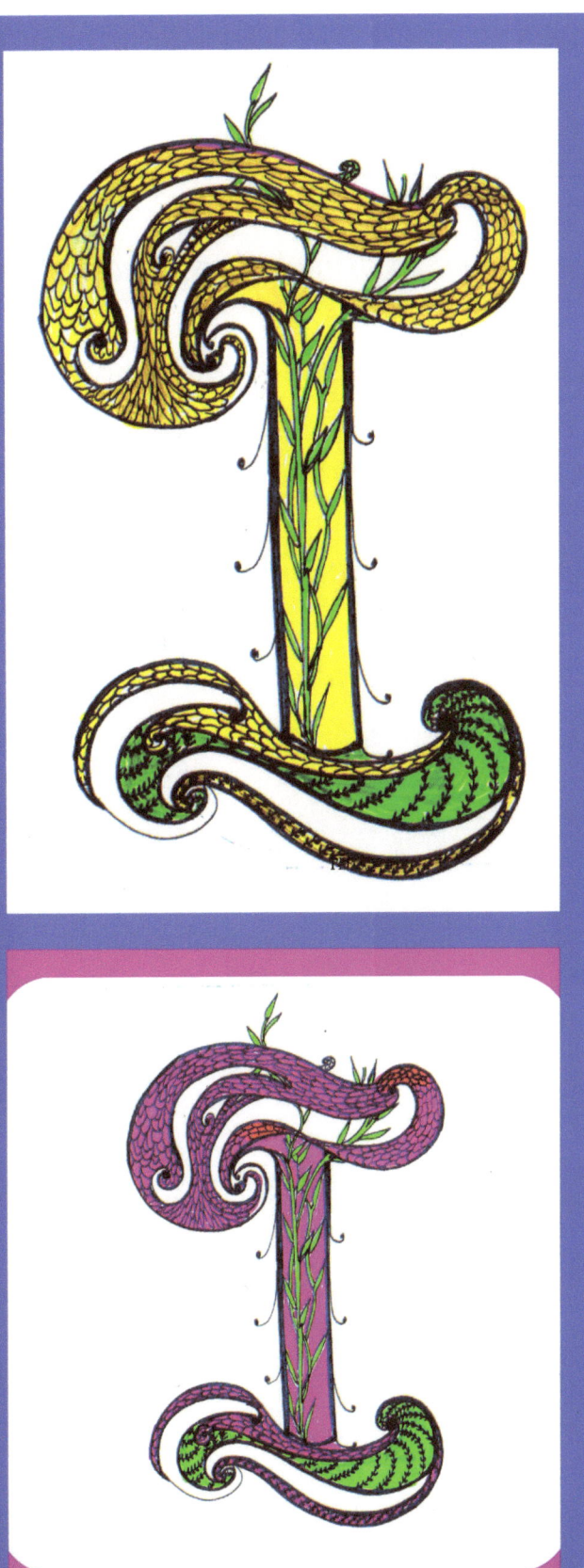

If you enjoyed the pages in this book I hope you will check out the other Letter Books available in this series. Hopefully you will be inspired on your own to draw letters of your own design or color in many new ways. Above all enjoy yourself!

Color to unwind, to be inspired, or to expand your coloring experience. Color till your heart's content. You never know when a special 1 might be just what you need.